THE BLESSING OF RAISING CHILDREN

SOPHIE BEMBA

Contents

Aknowledgments   v

Introduction   vii
By Sophie Bemba

1. The Gift In Every Child   1
2. Parenting As A Mission, Not A Routine   11
3. Parenting With Purpose   27
4. Raising Children To Become Good Adults   35
5. Parenting In The Modern Age - Overcoming Today's Challenges   47
6. The Role Of Faith In Parenting   53
7. The Power Of Connection And Communication   59

About the Author   67
Contact   69

Aknowledgments

I thank God for His love and for giving me the strength to write this book destined to parents and future parents. Thank you, Lord, for supporting me throughout the writing process of this book.

I would also like to thank my parents, **Mr. Jean Rocil Bemba** and **Mrs. Pierrette Bemba**, for being a great inspiration in the education of children, and excellent role models in parenting.

Thank you to my brothers and sisters**: Bénédicte, Brice, Jude, Evrard, and Rolix**, for the bond we have shared since our childhood. Bond which greatly inspired me while writing this book.

A huge thank you to my husband, **Mr. Jean Bruno Kemoko,** whose support, love and constant presence, have allowed me to embrace successfully the parenting of our children, despite challenges.

A heartfelt thank you to my beloved children: **Youngui, Alycia, Képhie, Given, Louirette, Kiesse, and Mayela,** who bring me joy, honour, and the blessing of being a parent. Through them, I have come to understand, the depth and happiness of raising children successfully, as well as the blessing they represent in our lives as parents.

A special Thank you to **Pastor Errol Lawson**, whose book writing masterclass, enabled me to complete this masterpiece.

Thanks to these outstanding women, who have been encouraging me for several years to write books: **Mentor Béatrice Hingfène, Aunt Amélie Akouemo, and Mrs. Albertine Kokou.**

A special thanks to **Coach Siân Olivia Mafi-amba,** her support in the publication and successful launch of this book. Ensuring that it becomes a bestseller.

Introduction
THE SACRED CALL OF PARENTING
By Sophie Bemba

I come from a large family, where there were many of us at home, and we had a very fulfilling family life—close-knit and united. I noticed that whenever there were children around me, there was an attraction. There were moments of exchange, of complicity, and even sometimes jealousy from the mother's heart, seeing her child grow attached to me, seeing her child share moments with me. This made me dream one day of becoming a mother myself, of receiving this blessing, of having the grace to give birth. It was a dream, but since I was young, it remained just that—a dream. As time went on, I reached the point where I could say to myself, "I will get married, and I will have children," without knowing exactly what would follow or how it would all unfold.

The journey to motherhood shaped itself gradually. As I reached adulthood, I finished my studies, found a job, and started working. I began to ask myself questions, guided by my mother's traditional wisdom that a woman should be settled by her mid-twenties. While today's realities are different, those maternal words echoed in my mind as I built my career. I had comfort, I was well-settled, and I earned my money. But at that point, it was as if something was missing. It felt like something wasn't yet fulfilled. Then I met my fiancé, and together, we began planning our future. The desire to become parents grew stronger, and soon, I discovered the joyful surprise of pregnancy—a dream transforming into reality.

Pregnancy brought with it a profound transformation, both physical and mental. I discovered this strange and beautiful feeling of knowing that I was carrying life, realising that I needed to care not just for myself, but for this little being inside me. There was fear, being my first time, and with that came anxiety—the fear of falling, of hurting myself, of not being able to handle it all. Yet it was also a journey of immense joy.

I was fortunate to be well-supported, engaging in activities that helped me move beyond anxiety into appreciation of these magical moments. This time of anticipation also sparked practical growth—I even obtained my driver's license just a month before giving birth, knowing I would need it for this new chapter of life.

The day of my daughter's birth remains vivid in my memory. On January 13th, 2006, I woke up exhausted from the final weeks of pregnancy. By noon, the first contractions began—bearable at first, then increasingly intense. In those moments of anticipation and pain, I found myself connecting deeply with God, praying for a smooth delivery and a healthy baby. These were the last precious moments before my life would change forever.

On Friday the 13th, which is considered a lucky day in France, my daughter made her entrance into the world. There she was, in our hands, letting out her first cry, giving us her first look, and her first smile. These were magical moments of pure joy, the profound realisation that we had truly given life. Everything went well, but I quickly understood that life would never be the same. We now had this tiny person who needed all our attention and care. Every decision, every moment would now revolve around her wellbeing and future.

Looking back now, with seven children ranging from toddler to young adult, I understand that those first moments of motherhood were just the beginning of a profound mission. That Friday the 13th wasn't just about welcoming my first child—it was about stepping into a role that would require constant intention, purpose, and vision. Like many parents, I initially focused on surviving each day, managing routines, and meeting immediate needs. But over the years, I've discovered that parenting isn't just about managing daily tasks—it's about shaping futures, building character, and creating legacies that will impact generations to come.

This book is born from that discovery and the transformative journey that followed. Through these pages, I'll share not just what I've learned through raising seven unique individuals, but practical ways to transform your own parenting journey from routine to purpose, from survival to mission. Whether you're expecting your first child or navigating the teenage years, this book will guide you in embracing the profound purpose of parenting and the unique blessing each child brings to your family.

Together, we'll explore how to move beyond the daily challenges of parenting to discover the deeper joy and purpose in raising children who will make a positive impact on the world. We'll delve into practical strategies for intentional parenting, methods for recognising and nurturing each child's unique gifts, and ways to build a family legacy that will endure for generations. This isn't just another parenting manual—it's an invitation to view your role as a parent through new eyes and to embrace the sacred mission of raising children with purpose and vision.

The Gift In Every Child

Understanding the Profound Nature of Each Child

My journey into motherhood began in an unexpected way, teaching me my first profound lesson about the unique nature of every child. While most imagine their parenting journey starting in a delivery room, mine began with an eleven-year-old girl who had lost her biological mother. Through adopting her, I learned that motherhood transcends biological connections—it's about recognising and nurturing the unique spirit of each child who enters our lives.

Today, that daughter is twenty-four, and watching her grow has reinforced what I've come to understand as the foundation of purposeful parenting: every child arrives with their own special purpose and timing. This truth became even clearer as my family grew to include seven children, each bringing distinct gifts and opportunities that transformed our lives in ways I could never have anticipated.

The Unexpected Ways Children Bless Our Lives

When we think about the blessings children bring, we often focus on the obvious joys—first smiles, milestone achievements, and proud moments. However, my experience has revealed a deeper truth: children often catalyse growth and opportunity in surprisingly practical ways. With the birth of my 5th child, fourth daughter in 2011, I witnessed how a child's arrival can open unexpected doors. Each subsequent birth seemed to coincide with new possibilities—whether in marriage, career growth, or personal development.

Consider how my fifth child's arrival aligned with the opening of our first restaurant, or how our sixth child's birth preceded further business expansion. These weren't mere coincidences but demonstrations of how children can inspire us to grow, take risks, and discover capabilities we never knew we possessed. This pattern repeated itself throughout my journey, teaching me to look beyond the surface to recognise the multifaceted ways children enrich our lives.

The Divine Timing of Each Child

One of the most powerful lessons I've learned is about divine timing in parenting. After three daughters, I longed for a son, and when my fourth child—a boy—was born, it reinforced my understanding that each child arrives at precisely the right moment. Even our seventh child, conceived during the COVID-19 pandemic when I thought my family was complete, proved that life's greatest gifts often arrive unexpectedly.

This understanding of timing extends beyond just the sequence of births. Each child brings their own "season" of learning and growth. My experience with blended family dynamics, particularly when my husband joined us in France, showed how children can help forge stronger family bonds and create new opportunities for love and understanding to flourish.

Recognising Individual Gifts

Through raising seven unique individuals, I've observed how each child manifests their gifts differently. Some show their blessings through their ability to bring people together, others through their capacity to inspire change or innovation in those around them. My first adopted daughter, for instance, taught our family about resilience and the power of chosen love. Another child might demonstrate extraordinary empathy, while yet another shows remarkable problem-solving abilities.

The key to recognising these gifts lies in paying attention to the subtle ways each child influences their environment and the people around them. Sometimes these gifts appear in unexpected packages—a challenging child might be teaching us patience, while a quiet one might be showing us the power of observation and contemplation.

The Transformative Power of Parenthood

Parenthood transforms us in ways we can hardly imagine at the outset. Through each pregnancy and child, I've experienced growth not just emotionally and spiritually, but also in practical life skills and professional capabilities. This transformation requires patience, endurance, and the wisdom to embrace each season of life with its unique challenges and opportunities.

Understanding this transformative journey helps us approach parenting with greater purpose. When we recognise that each child brings not just responsibilities but also possibilities for growth, we can embrace our role with renewed enthusiasm and intentionality.

Creating a Legacy Through Our Children

The true blessing of having children extends far beyond our immediate family circle. Each child represents an opportunity to influence future generations positively. Through my experience with seven children, I've witnessed how the values we instil and the love we share ripples outward, affecting not just our family but our broader community.

Practical Applications for Parents

In my years of raising seven children and observing countless others, I've discovered several practical ways to recognise and nurture the unique gifts each child brings. Let me share some approaches that have proved invaluable in our family's journey.

Creating Space for Discovery

One of the most important things we can do as parents is to create an environment where children feel safe to explore their interests and abilities. In our home, this meant setting aside dedicated spaces for different activities—a quiet reading nook for our bookworm, an area for artistic expression for our creative souls, and space for physical activity for our more energetic children.

I remember how our sixth child showed an early

interest in cooking. Rather than dismissing this as a passing fancy, we adjusted our kitchen setup to allow him safe participation in meal preparation. Today, at age twelve, he often prepares family meals, displaying a natural talent for combining flavours that none of his siblings share.

The Art of Observation

Careful observation forms the cornerstone of understanding our children's unique gifts. This involves more than merely watching; it requires mindful attention to patterns in their behaviour, preferences, and ways of interacting with the world. Consider keeping a simple journal to note these observations—you might be surprised by the insights that emerge over time.

For instance, I noticed that my second youngest would often solve conflicts between siblings before I even became aware of them. This observation helped us nurture her natural diplomatic abilities, and we now often seek her perspective when family decisions need to be made.

Supporting Different Learning Styles

Each child approaches learning differently, and recognising these differences proves crucial in nurturing their gifts. Some of my children grasp concepts best through hands-on experience, whilst others prefer reading or verbal instruction. Understanding and supporting these different learning styles helps each child flourish in their unique way.

Embracing the Challenges

It's important to acknowledge that recognising and nurturing individual gifts isn't always straightforward. Sometimes, what we initially perceive as challenging behaviour might actually signal a unique gift trying to express itself. My fifth child's constant questioning and curiosity, which could sometimes feel overwhelming, ultimately revealed a brilliant analytical mind.

Building Family Unity Through Diversity

One beautiful aspect of having children with different gifts is the opportunity to build family unity through these differences. In our home, we've established a practice we call 'Talent Share Sundays', where each child takes turns teaching something they're good at to their siblings. This not only validates their unique abilities but also helps everyone appreciate each other's strengths.

Reflection questions for parents

Consider these questions as you think about your own children's unique gifts:

What activities seem to energise your child, making them lose track of time?

In what situations does your child show natural leadership or initiative?

What kinds of problems does your child solve effortlessly, perhaps without even realising it?

How does your child prefer to receive and express love?

What activities or subjects spark your child's curiosity and generate endless questions?

Moving Forward

As we conclude this chapter, I encourage you to take time this week to observe your children with fresh eyes. Look beyond the obvious talents to discover the subtle gifts that make each child unique. Remember, these gifts might not always align with our expectations or society's standard measures of success.

Consider starting a 'Gift Journal' where you can record your observations about each child's unique qualities and the ways they bless your family. This practice not only helps us remain mindful of our children's individual gifts but also provides a beautiful record of their development over time.

In the next chapter, we'll explore how to transform daily parenting routines into purposeful opportunities for nurturing these gifts. We'll discuss practical strategies for incorporating this awareness into everyday life, ensuring that our recognition of each child's unique qualities shapes our parenting approach in meaningful ways.

A Final Thought

Remember, recognising and nurturing our children's gifts isn't about pushing them toward particular achievements or comparing them with others. Rather, it's about creating an environment where each child feels valued for who they are and supported in becoming who they're meant to be. As we move forward in our parenting journey, let's carry this understanding close to our hearts, allowing it to guide our daily interactions and long-term aspirations for our children.

2

Parenting As A Mission, Not A Routine

The Journey of Transformation

When my husband and I decided to blend our families and move to England, we faced what appeared to be insurmountable challenges. I left behind a comfortable life in France—a good job, my own flat, and an established routine—to step into the unknown. Neither speaking English nor understanding the culture, I found myself in a foreign land with a growing family to nurture. This transition taught me my first crucial lesson about purposeful parenting: true parenting often requires us to step beyond our comfort zones for the greater good of our children.

Embracing Change with Purpose

The decision to relocate wasn't merely about geographical movement; it represented a fundamental shift in how we approached parenting. My husband and I had met years before—when I was 16 and he was 21—but life had taken us on separate journeys. When we reconnected and married in Birmingham on 23rd August 2008, we knew we were embarking on more than just a marriage; we were accepting a mission to create a unified family from our blended circumstances.

The Reality of Purposeful Parenting

Our family grew rapidly after our wedding. Within months, I gave birth to our second daughter in October, and suddenly, the theoretical challenges of parenting became very real indeed. Here I was, in a foreign country, without family support, unable to speak the language, facing the daily challenges of raising children. This experience taught me that parenting as a mission requires:

1. Adaptability: Learning to thrive in new circumstances

2. Resilience: Pushing through language and cultural barriers

3. Vision: Seeing beyond immediate challenges to long-term family goals.

From Survival to Strategy

By 2010, with the birth of our son and shortly after, another daughter in 2011, our home bustled with five children ranging from newborns to pre-teens. This period taught me that effective parenting requires moving beyond mere survival to strategic planning:

- Creating structured routines whilst maintaining flexibility
- Developing systems for managing multiple schedules
- Building support networks through community and church
- Balancing individual attention with family unity

The Business of Family Life

In 2009, we took another leap of faith by opening our first business—an off-licence shop. This venture, later transformed into a restaurant, presented new challenges in balancing work and family life. Some days I found myself in the shop with my youngest child whilst the older ones were at school. These experiences taught me valuable lessons about:

- Integration of family and work responsibilities

- Teaching children the value of work through example
- Making difficult choices for the family's well being
- Recognising when to pivot for the sake of family priorities

Building Community in the Midst of Change

Without extended family nearby, we learned to create our own support system. Our church became our extended family, offering strength and encouragement when we needed it most. This experience highlighted the importance of:
- Seeking and building community
- Teaching children the value of relationships beyond immediate family
- Finding strength in faith and shared values
- Creating stability amidst change

Practical Strategies for Purposeful Parenting

Through these experiences, I developed several practical approaches that transformed our daily routines into purposeful parenting moments:
1. **Morning Planning Ritual**
- Setting daily intentions for each child
- Creating space for individual connections
- Anticipating and preparing for challenges

2. **Communication Framework**
- Regular family meetings
- One-on-one time with each child
- Open discussions about changes and challenges

3. **Cultural Integration Strategies**
- Embracing new experiences as a family
- Maintaining important cultural traditions
- Creating our own unique family culture

The Mission Continues

Today, as I reflect on our journey, I see how each challenge shaped our family's mission. Parenting isn't just about managing daily tasks—it's about intentionally building a legacy that will impact generations. Every decision, from moving countries to closing a business, has been guided by this greater purpose.

Parenting Is a Mission with Vision

In this part of our journey, I want to highlight the importance of parenting with vision. Today, having children shouldn't be just about fulfilling a personal desire or achieving independence. It's about understanding the deeper purpose behind parenthood.

Raising children is more than the physical act of becoming a mother or father. It is a mission full of meaning. This is one of the key reasons for writing this book—because through my own journey of becoming a parent and raising children, I have come to deeply appreciate the weight and purpose of parenting.

You see, my husband and I both come from large families. While this gave us familiarity with children and family dynamics, it wasn't enough to prepare us for the real work of parenting. Becoming a parent requires vision, mission, and a strong sense of responsibility. No one is born knowing how to parent—we grow into it, and it's a process of continuous learning.

Yes, our upbringing contributes to the way we parent. The family environments we grew up in, the values we were taught—all of that plays a role. But when it's your turn to raise children, you must build a solid foundation. You need a vision for your family. You must ask: What kind of future am I building for my children? What values do I want to pass on?

Sadly, many families today are losing sight of this. Many parents don't realise the God-given mission they've been entrusted with. The Bible tells us in Psalm 127:3-4, "Children are a heritage from the Lord, offspring a reward from him. Like arrows in the hands of a warrior are children born in one's youth." This shows that children are a gift from God, and we, as parents, are like archers, guiding our children carefully and intentionally toward their destinies.

God entrusts us with these children for a time. He loans them to us, and it's our responsibility to guide them according to the vision He has for them. And for that to happen, we, as parents, must also carry a vision —one that aligns with God's purpose for their lives.

This begins with being:

A present parent

A guiding parent

A parent who lays strong foundations

Unfortunately, many parents today are letting go of this mission. Whether they already have children or are preparing for them in the future, it's important to recognise that parenting is the most important mission God placed on this earth. Before any career, achievement, or title, family is the first and most sacred assignment.

This mission requires strength, unity, and intentionality. Many parents are not aligned when it comes to how they raise their children. They don't share a clear vision. But we must be examples to our children and understand that they've been entrusted to us for a reason.

As a Christian, I can't help but emphasise the importance of raising our children to know and walk with God. The Bible says in Proverbs 22:6, "Train up a child in the way he should go, and when he is old, he will not depart from it." Parenting with vision means teaching divine principles and walking alongside our children as they discover their purpose.

Even for those who are not Christians, there is still

a universal path to follow when you become a parent. The moment you give life, you have a responsibility—to educate, guide, nurture, and shape that life into someone who contributes positively to society.

When I followed my husband to England, I found myself in a foreign land. I didn't speak the language. I had no family. The only person I could trust was my husband. I began raising children in a culture I didn't know, in a language I didn't understand.

Both my husband and I come from a French-speaking background, originally from Congo-Brazzaville. I was born in France, spent part of my childhood there, and another part back in Congo when my parents returned for work. My husband was born and raised in Congo and later moved to South Africa as an adult, where he was influenced by an English-speaking, South African culture.

We reconnected years later, after having been childhood friends. I was 16 when we met, and he was 21, just starting university. Our friendship grew, and eventually, he proposed. He came to France for a visit but didn't feel settled—he preferred the English-speaking environment. So, we made the decision to start our life together in England. We got married and began our family in a completely new country.

.   .   .

THIS TRANSITION CAME with major challenges. I had to learn the language, adapt to the culture, and start over with no family network. When my parents were still in Africa, I couldn't lean on them for help. I had grown up surrounded by cousins and extended family, but now I was responsible for my own children —my own blood. That made everything different.

I had looked after my younger sister, cousins, and other children growing up, but now, as a mother to my own children, I realised that this was something else entirely. This was my child—my flesh and blood, a soul entrusted to me by God. And I had to rise to the calling.

As a couple, we also needed to agree on a shared vision for parenting. My husband had his upbringing, and I had mine. We had to merge our perspectives, align our values, and find unity in how we raised our children.

By God's grace, we were both raised in Christian homes, which gave us common ground. But it wasn't always easy—we had to grow spiritually and mature in our faith to fully embrace the mission of raising children together. From the start, we decided to raise our children with Christian values, faith, and love. We wanted to pass on a legacy of faith that would endure across generations.

We also committed to raising children who are united and rooted, despite living in a foreign land. We had to blend cultures, balance traditions, and prepare our children to thrive in a world that was very different from the one we came from. That meant adapting, learning, and staying focused on building a strong future for our family.

Today, we must recognise that having children is not just about giving birth—it's about purpose. In some communities, particularly among the younger generation, there is a worrying mindset: the idea that having a child is a pathway to personal gain—whether for independence, housing, financial benefits, or escaping a difficult family situation.

Some young women, for example, believe that becoming pregnant will help them leave their parents' home and gain autonomy. Others, especially those coming from poorer backgrounds, may see having a child with a financially supportive man as a way to improve their living conditions. But these reasons are misguided.

Having a child should never be about convenience or escape. Children are not tools—they are souls with destinies. Becoming a parent must be a conscious and sacred decision, rooted in love, responsibility, and vision.

Parenthood has a very specific purpose. It's about building a society where we understand the power and responsibility we have as parents. Having a family is not random—it is part of a divine plan. That purpose includes guiding children, giving them time, walking with them through life, nurturing their gifts, helping them grow in character and competence, and educating them to thrive.

Unfortunately, in today's fast-paced world, many parents have children and then dive straight into work or personal ambition. I speak to mothers—and fathers too—who become consumed by their careers, working endlessly while their children receive little attention or presence.

When you decide to have children, you must also decide to give them your time and your heart. Parenting requires balance. Each parent must play their role—fathers and mothers alike—and the success of a family lies in both sides embracing that role intentionally.

It is through time—time spent together, time listening, laughing, learning—that we pass on values. It's in those daily interactions that our children absorb the principles they will carry into adulthood. If we don't give them this, they may grow up disconnected and confused about who they are.

I've lived this tension myself. As a self-employed woman running a business, I worked full time. When I launched my salon, I poured in hours upon hours. Some nights I was there late—with the children beside me. Eventually, this imbalance began to impact my family. My husband shared how he felt—how I was giving too much to work and not enough to the children or to him.

That was when I heard the gentle whisper of God. He reminded me that while my work mattered, my children needed me more. And yes, I took my husband's words seriously. The children were still very young, and I realised I was missing irreplaceable moments. I needed to make a change—not to stop working, but to restructure how I worked.

So, I began to reorganise my life and business. It wasn't an overnight fix—it took months of small decisions, consistent effort, and prayer. But I started finding balance. From 2022 into 2023, things began to fall into place.

I cut back a few hours at the salon. I built a second stream of income by offering online coaching, which allowed me to work more flexibly while still being present at home.

And I want to highlight this: I also sought training —not just business training, but coaching and mentorship on how to be a better wife, mother, and parent. That formation opened my eyes and helped me understand that parenting isn't just a season—it's a divine mission.

Being a parent is not just about survival or routine. It is about purpose. It's about vision. And it is about living out the responsibility that God has given us—to raise children who walk in truth, who understand love, and who will carry light into the world.

REFLECTION QUESTIONS AND PRACTICAL EXERCISE

Take a moment to consider these questions about your own parenting journey:

1. **Purpose and Vision**

- What core values guide your family's daily decisions?

- How do your current routines align with your long-term vision for your children?

- What legacy do you hope to create through your parenting?

2. **Change and adaptation**

- What significant changes has parenthood brought to your life?

- How have you grown through these changes?

- Which challenges have shaped your approach to parenting?

3. **Family culture**

- What traditions or practices make your family unique?

- How do you balance different cultural influences in your home?
- What rituals bring your family closer together?

PRACTICAL EXERCISES FOR PURPOSEFUL PARENTING

1. The Family Mission Statement Exercise

GATHER your family and create a mission statement together:
- What matters most to us as a family?
- How do we want to treat each other?
- What do we want to achieve together?
- What values define us?

Write these down and display them prominently in your home.

2. Daily Purpose Planner

Create a simple template to transform routine moments into purposeful interactions:

Morning:
- One specific way to connect with each child
- A value or lesson to emphasise today
- A moment to create together

EVENING
- What went well today?
- What could we do differently tomorrow?
- What did we learn as a family?

3. Cultural Heritage Map

Draw a family tree that includes:
- Important family traditions
- Cultural celebrations
- Special recipes
- Family stories to pass down

NB: Use this as a teaching tool with your children.

Action Steps for the Week Ahead

1. Monday: Observe your current family routines. Which ones feel purposeful? Which need adjustment?

2. Tuesday: Have a family meeting to discuss one change you'd like to make together.

3. Wednesday: Create a visual reminder of your family's core values.

4. Thursday: Spend ten minutes with each child, learning about their hopes and dreams.

5. Friday: Review your week. What moments felt most meaningful?

6. Weekend: Plan one activity that builds your family's unique culture.

. . .

REMEMBER, transforming parenting from routine to mission doesn't happen overnight. It's a gradual process of intentional choices and consistent effort. Start with small changes, celebrate progress, and keep your larger purpose in mind.

As we move forward to Chapter 3, we'll explore how to develop character and values in our children whilst maintaining the unique essence of each child's personality.

Chapter Summary

- Parenting as a mission requires vision beyond daily tasks

    - Embracing change creates opportunities for growth

    - Building strong family cultures supports purposeful parenting

    - Community and support networks strengthen family life

    - Intentional planning transforms routine moments into meaningful experiences

Parenting With Purpose

Hello and welcome! In this third chapter, we'll talk about what it means to raise a child with purpose. Today, being a parent isn't just about saying, "I want to have a child." In many parts of society—especially among young people—we've observed a trend where some want to become pregnant simply as a way to gain independence.

In parts of Europe, for example, some young women seek pregnancy as a path toward receiving benefits, leaving their parents' homes, getting a flat, or having access to some financial support. Others come from difficult backgrounds and see pregnancy as a way to escape poverty—perhaps by having a child with a man who provides for them. But these motivations often lack vision and are ultimately short-sighted.

Having a child must be purposeful. The goal

should be to raise that child with care, walk with them through life, help develop their talents and skills, and guide them with values. Too often, we see parents—mothers and fathers alike—who have children and then dive straight into work, often without truly preparing for the time, patience, and balance that family life requires.

When you decide to have a family, it demands a shared responsibility, with each parent playing their role intentionally. Parenting requires time, attention, and dedication, especially when it comes to instilling values. It is in the time we spend with our children that we are able to pass on what truly matters.

In my own journey, I've experienced this tension first-hand. I was running a business—self-employed, working long hours in my hair salon. There were many nights I stayed late at the salon with the children. Eventually, it began to affect my marriage. My husband felt that I was pouring too much of myself into the business and not enough into the family—into him or the children.

AND THEN CAME the whisper of God, gently prompting me to reflect. My husband's words also hit home. The children were still young, and I was missing vital moments. I realised that something had to change. It wasn't about quitting work altogether but rather learning to balance entrepreneurship with motherhood.

This wasn't an overnight change. It took time—months, even years. But I began to restructure my life and business. By 2022 and especially 2023, I finally found a rhythm that allowed me to combine my physical business with a new venture: online coaching. I learned how to work smarter, not longer, and how to build routines that served both my clients and my children.

I also sought training to better understand my role—not just as a mother, but as a wife, a parent, and a leader in my home. That education opened my eyes to the true mission of parenting—not just falling into a routine, but living out a vision.

As children of God, we are given the divine responsibility of raising human beings. We are entrusted with guiding them into adulthood so that they, in turn, can make an impact in society and carry forward the vision of humanity.

To do this well, we must spend time with them—enough time to notice their hidden gifts, their talents, their potential—and then nurture those things. This requires intentional routines, built around love, discipline, and consistency.

For example, in our home, we prioritise time around the table. We switch off devices and talk. We laugh, share stories, play games, and tell our children about our own youth. We pass on values through these moments. And we can already see the fruit of that.

Our eldest daughter works full-time and is thriving. Our second is in her first year of university and works part-time. They both reflect the values we have consistently shared with them.

As for our younger five children who are still in school, we continue the same approach—speaking life into them daily, helping them develop character, and walking with them as they grow.

I've seen first-hand how giving time to our children protects them and guides their choices. For instance, with our son, now 15, we noticed something change when he was in Year 8.

Through spending time with him, dropping him off at school, and observing his behaviour, we discovered that he was beginning to be influenced by peers who were engaging in negative behaviours—smoking, inappropriate relationships, and heavy conversations for that age.

Because we were present, we caught it early. And because we had already invested time and built trust, we were able to correct, support, and guide him back on track.

REFLECTION QUESTIONS

1. What was your motivation for becoming a parent?

Was it intentional, or did you discover the purpose along the way?

2. Do you currently have a clear vision for your family?

If yes, write it down. If not, what would you like that vision to be?

3. How much quality time do you spend with your children each week?

What activities or moments do you share intentionally?

4. What values do you want to instil in your children?

How are you currently modelling those values in your daily life?

5. In what ways does your work or daily routine impact your availability to your children?

Are there any adjustments you feel prompted to make?

6. When was the last time you had a meaningful, uninterrupted conversation with your child?

What did you learn from that moment?

PRACTICAL EXERCISES

1. Create a Family Vision Statement

– Sit down with your spouse or by yourself and write a short statement that defines what you want your family to represent and build toward.

– Example: "Our family is a place of love, growth, faith, and support. We raise responsible and kind individuals who contribute positively to the world."

2. Schedule a Weekly 'Family Table Time'

– Choose one evening per week where all screens are turned off, and everyone sits around the table for food, laughter, stories, or games.

– Let each family member share a highlight or challenge from their week.

3. Time Audit

– For three days, track how much time you spend working, on your phone, doing chores, and with your children.

– Reflect on what you discover and ask: Where can I make space for more intentional parenting?

4. Talent Spotting

– Choose one child this week and observe their interests, habits, and strengths.

– Write down at least two potential talents or gifts you've noticed and find one small way to nurture them.

5. Parent Check-In with Your Partner

– If you're parenting with a spouse, plan a time to check in:

– Are we aligned on our parenting vision?

– Are we supporting each other's roles in the home?

– What adjustments can we make together?

6. Prayer or Meditation Time

– Set aside 5–10 minutes daily to pray or meditate for wisdom, patience, and guidance in parenting.

– Use this time to centre yourself before stepping into the day.

4

Raising Children To Become
Good Adults

A good adult is not defined by how much money they earn, how perfect they appear, or the titles they hold. A good adult is someone with character, a strong sense of responsibility, and the ability to love and lead well. As parents, our mission is to raise children who grow into such adults.

We must never forget that before we became parents, we were children too—inspired and influenced by our own parents. That's why it's essential to strive to be good adults, capable of inspiring through our example: our conduct, our responsibilities, and our ability to give love and sound guidance.

Every child will eventually grow into an adult. Our responsibility is to prepare them to be emotionally secure, resilient, and compassionate. We must raise them to have character, a sense of purpose, and the ability to build and lead their future homes and families with integrity and wisdom.

These qualities don't develop overnight. Becoming a parent doesn't automatically make us experts. We grow into parenthood just as we grew into adulthood. We draw from what we learned as children, and from the values passed on to us. That's why I want to honour my own parents.

My father, now 85, and my mother, 75, gave me the stability and emotional grounding that I now try to pass on to my own children. I thank them from the bottom of my heart.

Still, I had to learn many things on my own—especially because I raised my children in the UK, far from my family. When I arrived here, it was my husband who brought me over. I raised my children without immediate family support—no parents, no siblings nearby—only my husband. That is why I often speak about him. The two of us had to forge a path together as parents. We learned. We made mistakes. We grew.

Raising children without a support network is hard, especially when you come from a culture where family is central—whether in African or European traditions. Normally, we'd rely on parents, siblings, and relatives. But we didn't have that. We had to build everything ourselves. Yes, I could call my mother for advice, but day-to-day parenting was ours to carry.

What I've learned is this: the roots of success start at home. Schools can educate, but the real foundations —principles, discipline, love, and vision—are taught at home. Children who grow up in a secure, encouraging, and value-driven environment learn how to manage conflict, pursue goals, and develop emotional strength.

Let me share an example. We have two daughters —one is 24, the other 19. Recently, we saw clear evidence of the values we've passed on. This past Christmas (2024), they surprised us in the most beautiful way. Without being asked, they organised gifts for their younger siblings—and for us. From their own earnings, they chose to bless their family. That moment touched our hearts deeply. We saw the fruits of our labour. We saw that they had taken on responsibility with joy and maturity.

It's in these small, powerful gestures that we see the value of the principles we've instilled—principles of love, unity, generosity, and leadership. There have been times when we weren't at home, and our daughters stepped up.

They cooked, took care of their siblings, went shopping—without hesitation. Their bond with their siblings is strong and genuine. And this reflects our intentional effort to build a united, God-centred family.

We are a Christian family, and we teach our children to walk with God. Our faith has helped my husband and me stay united and focused in our parenting. It has strengthened our marriage and shaped our children's outlook on life. We know, without a doubt, that our older daughters will one day be wonderful wives and mothers, just as they've already shown themselves to be trustworthy, caring, and grounded.

Now, we continue this same work with our five younger children. We're teaching them to manage conflict, pursue their goals, and develop inner discipline. We constantly affirm them, challenge them, and encourage deep, meaningful relationships among themselves.

This strong foundation helps them become thriving, well-adjusted adults—not just in their careers but in their future homes, marriages, and roles in society. That is the true mission of parenting: not just to raise happy children, but to raise healthy, whole, purposeful adults.

The more intentional we are in our parenting, the more likely our children are to become adults who are joyful, clear in purpose, and emotionally rich. Not just financially successful—but spiritually, emotionally, and socially rich.

This book is written to remind us of the joy and sacredness of parenting, and the importance of investing in our children. Parenting is about building a legacy—a lasting inheritance that goes far beyond material things. We don't just pass on our DNA—we pass on values, principles, and a sense of mission.

Parenting is a generational work. What we teach our children, they will pass on to their children, and so on. It's a never-ending chain. That's why we must embrace the role of parent with a full heart, knowing that it is a powerful calling.

When we take this role seriously, we give our children a roadmap for life—a blueprint they can follow and eventually pass down. This legacy is one of vision, strength, and purpose. As parents, we have no excuse. We must rise to this task. It's not just about our own homes—it's about shaping society.

Healthy, whole adults contribute to healthier, stronger communities. They become mentors, leaders, and compassionate voices in a world that desperately needs healing. That's why I wrote this book—to stir a renewed sense of purpose in parents. To awaken hearts. To remind us that we are not alone—and that, yes, we can succeed in this mission.

And if you feel unprepared, take heart: you can learn. Becoming a good adult, and a good parent, is a journey. It's something we can grow into. This is not just a personal mission—it's a contribution to the future of society.

By defining and modelling what a good adult looks like, we are shaping a better world for tomorrow. That is my hope for every parent and future parent reading this book: that you will discover the blessing and joy of raising children, and embrace your mission with confidence and love.

OUR CHILDREN ARE the adults of tomorrow. And tomorrow's adults are the foundation for the generations that follow. Let's build well.

You can ask for advice over the phone, speak with your mother, or get support from friends, but nothing replaces hands-on experience. For me, I'm grateful to God because I had the blessing of growing up in a large family.

I was born in France, but I spent much of my childhood in Congo before returning to France later. What stands out to me most from those years is growing up surrounded by cousins, aunts, uncles— always around family. I witnessed many births. I saw how children were raised. I helped care for my little sister—feeding her, bathing her, looking after her when our mum was at work.

I also helped care for my young cousins when my aunts had babies. This early exposure gave me a kind of informal training that became a great help when I became a mother myself. It gave me a head start and taught me what it meant to care for children practically.

But of course, pregnancy itself was a new and

emotional experience. I remember being afraid during my first pregnancy. I didn't fully understand what it would feel like. I'd seen others go through it, but living it myself was something completely different. I had fears—silly ones now, like being scared to walk in case I fell and hurt the baby.

But through it all, motherhood awakened something natural in me. And I believe that for most women, that maternal instinct does kick in. Still, it helps enormously to have had a strong foundation—a solid childhood, emotional stability, and loving family roots.

Growing up in a home full of love gives you the tools to become a strong parent. The family values you inherit—consistency, encouragement, structure—are things you pass on naturally. I remember how my parents and grandparents always encouraged us to learn, to be responsible, to contribute.

My husband had a similar experience. He too came from a home where strong values were taught. He's especially passionate about cleanliness and order. He's neat and precise—and he passes those standards on to our children. These are the kinds of values that matter:

Personal hygiene
Tidiness
Cooking and self-care

Intelligence and discipline
Giving your best in all things

These values are not automatic—they are learned. They're built over time, modelled and repeated. And now, we are intentional about passing them on to our children, just as they were passed to us.

But what if you didn't grow up in that kind of home? What if you didn't have that strong family foundation?

I want to tell you something important: it's never too late to learn. Even if your upbringing lacked structure or stability, you have the opportunity—right now —to break the cycle. You can become a different kind of parent. You can learn new ways.

This book, written in 2025, exists to encourage you, wherever you are in your parenting journey. Be open. Learn. Grow. Parenting can be learned. Being a good adult can be learned. It all starts with a decision.

Because before we can pass anything meaningful on to our children, we must first become that kind of adult ourselves. We must be healed, whole, and grounded. It starts with us.

CLOSING REFLECTION: THE POWER OF EARLY INSTRUCTION

To close this chapter, I want to share a powerful verse

from the Bible—one that brings clarity and spiritual weight to everything we've spoken about:

"Train up a child in the way he should go, and when he is old, he will not depart from it."
– Proverbs 22:6

What a promise.

THIS VERSE CAPTURES the heart of our message in Chapter 4. The Word of God confirms just how important it is to instruct our children in the way they should go. The emphasis is not just on teaching, but on intentional, directional instruction—guiding them with love, wisdom, and vision.

When we lay strong foundations in childhood—by shaping their character, imparting values, and creating a legacy—they carry those lessons into adulthood. This verse underlines the lasting impact of parenting done with purpose and faith.

It's a call to all of us—to start early, to be intentional, and to trust that what we plant today will bear fruit tomorrow. It reminds us that the efforts we make now are not in vain. They echo into the future.

May this scripture be a light for every family, and may it bless and inspire you to continue walking in your mission with strength, joy, and purpose.

Be abundantly blessed.

Thank you for sharing Chapter 5. Here's a

polished English translation of the full chapter, formatted for inclusion in the manuscript of A Legacy in Every Child: The Purpose and Power of Parenting.

REFLECTION QUESTIONS

1. How do you currently define a "good adult"? What values or traits stand out to you?

2. Reflect on your own upbringing—what positive values or character traits did your parents instil in you?

3. What aspects of your character do you hope to pass on to your children?

4. Are there areas in your parenting where you feel you're just "getting by" rather than being intentional?

5. What does legacy mean to you? How are you building one through your parenting?

PRACTICAL EXERCISES

Family Legacy Tree: Create a simple diagram showing the values, traditions, and lessons passed down from your parents. Then add what you are passing (or want to pass) on to your children.

Affirmation Practice: Write down five positive traits you see in each of your children. Read them aloud to your child during a quiet moment this week.

Character Challenge:

Pick one value (e.g. responsibility, kindness,

resilience) and create a weekly "challenge" with your child to practise that value. Reflect together at the end of the week.

Faith Conversation: If you are a person of faith, spend some time discussing a Bible verse or story that illustrates godly character. If not, select a meaningful proverb or quote to reflect on together.

5

Parenting In The Modern Age - Overcoming Today's Challenges

Parenting in today's world is not easy

Raising children in a technology-driven age, in a world filled with noise, distractions, and social pressures, is no small task. While our own parents certainly faced challenges in their time, the context has changed drastically. The digital era brings with it a flood of information, constant notifications, and ever-increasing societal demands. Parents today must navigate a world that never stops moving.

With several children of our own, we've felt this pressure firsthand. The pace is relentless. Social expectations are high. And on top of it all, it often feels like society gives more rights to children than to parents. In some Western cultures, for example, many parents fear the involvement of social services. Disciplining a child (not physically, but through firm guidance and boundaries) is sometimes viewed with suspicion, making parents hesitant to lead as they should.

But let me say this clearly: children need guidance, structure, love, and discipline. Our role as parents is not to be passive observers but to actively nurture, direct, and protect our children. A child without boundaries is a child at risk.

That's why teaching resilience is vital in the modern age. Just as we adults must learn to handle disappointment and uncertainty with strength and grace, so must our children. But they won't learn it on their own—they'll learn it by watching us. They imitate our courage, our adaptability, our attitude towards life. We must be their role models.

As a mother, I made a conscious choice to build a life that allowed me flexibility—to work for myself so I could be present for my children. That's been one of the best decisions of my life.

Because while financial success matters, true wealth lies in the values we pass on, in the love we share, and in the foundation, we build at home.

We've seen this bear fruit in our daughters. Our eldest now works full-time and is thriving in her career. Our second is finishing her first year of university while working part-time. They are grounded, responsible, and focused—because they were raised with purpose.

But it all starts with us. We must first develop ourselves. As parents, our personal growth matters. When we become better adults, we become better parents. Self-care, emotional stability, and spiritual growth aren't luxuries—they're necessary. They allow us to give more, love deeper, and create balanced homes.

Our home, for example, became a refuge from the chaos of the outside world. My husband and I have faced our share of challenges with the children, but our unity has helped us overcome so much. And while perfection isn't the goal, being present is. Presence matters.

A few years ago, my husband gave mobile phones to all our children. We quickly noticed that the family dynamic started to shift. Everyone was absorbed in their screens. Communication declined. So, we set new boundaries: no phones during the night, and all devices returned after school. Instead, we spent time together—playing board games, talking, watching films, dancing, sharing stories from our childhoods, and simply enjoying each other.

These daily moments helped our children open up. They felt heard. They shared their worries. We became aware of things they may not have realised were dangerous or unhealthy. Communication is key.

We also made sure our spiritual life was part of our family culture. We've raised our children in church, the same church where my husband and I were married in 2008. Sundays are family days—prayer, fellowship, maybe a meal out, a walk, a museum visit, or a fun outing. These shared experiences create memories that shape who they are.

And you know what? It doesn't take a lot of money to do this. What it takes is time. And intentionality.

FOR PARENTS WORKING full-time or single parents, I encourage you to think creatively. Maybe there's a side business or a flexible role that allows more time with your children. I believe our children are our first and most important "business." If we lose them while chasing wealth, what do we really gain?

Let's not hand our children over to the world. Let's raise them ourselves—with love, discipline, wisdom, and vision.

Yes, there are days we may doubt ourselves. We wonder: Am I doing enough? Am I good enough? But remember: there is no single perfect way to parent. What matters is your presence, your effort, and the foundation you're building each day.

We've learned to keep our children close—especially when we've seen the consequences of letting them be too influenced by their environment. We've had seasons where we allowed our children to mingle with local neighbours, only to see behavioural issues and misunderstandings arise. We quickly adjusted. We communicated clearly with our children and explained why we were making changes. And because we've always fostered trust and presence, they listened.

Even now, we're intentional with every outing, every gathering. We manage time. We stay involved. We know where they are and who they're with. Not because we want to control them—but because we care.

Being present reassures a child. It gives them confidence. It anchors them in a world that often feels uncertain.

This is the heart of parenting in the modern age: staying grounded in values, resilient in challenges, and present through it all.

REFLECTION QUESTIONS

1. In what ways has modern technology affected your relationship with your children—for better or worse?

2. How do you personally manage digital distractions in your home? Could any boundaries be strengthened?

3. Are you present enough in your child's daily life to know what is really happening in their heart and world?

4. What pressures do you face as a modern parent, and how do you cope with them?

5. What practical steps can you take to make your home a peaceful and nurturing refuge for your children?

PRACTICAL EXERCISES

Digital Detox Evening

Choose one evening this week to turn off all screens and spend uninterrupted time with your children. Play games, share stories, or cook a meal together.

Family Meeting: Host a casual family discussion to ask your children how they feel about their current routines, screen time, or what they wish they had more of from you.

Stress Journal

Keep a short daily journal of moments where you feel stressed and how you react—then reflect on how you can model emotional regulation more effectively.

Vision Board

As a family, create a vision board for your home life. Include words, pictures, and goals that represent the kind of atmosphere you want to build together.

Spiritual Health Check-In

If applicable, take time to pray or reflect with your children, asking them how they feel spiritually and what questions they might have about faith or values.

6

The Role Of Faith In Parenting

The role of faith in parenting is, in my view, essential. Faith is the cornerstone of Christian parenting, but it also has a powerful impact, even for those who don't necessarily identify as Christians. One way or another, we all operate with some form of faith.

As a Christian family, I've come to realise that raising children without this spiritual foundation can be quite challenging. Raising children in faith is not limited to just going to church. It's about creating a Christ-centred home where God's presence is experienced daily. For instance, although we used to go to church regularly, our son's football matches – which often take place on Sundays – now require my husband and me to alternate. So, we established a system of praying together at home, especially in the evenings and on weekends, including Bible reading and watching Christian films as a family.

I'm reminded of Proverbs 22:6: "Train up a child in the way he should go; and when he is old, he will not depart from it." This verse shows us that parenting is not just a responsibility – it's a spiritual mission.

Parents are called to guide their children in discovering a personal relationship with God, encouraging them to pray, study the Bible, and worship. In our home, we have regular worship moments. I love gospel music, and we incorporate it into our family devotion time. Just this morning, my four-year-old daughter was singing one of our prayer songs, and it truly warmed my heart. It's clear that, little by little, these spiritual seeds are being planted and taking root.

This spiritual discipline shapes a child's character, values, and life choices. By teaching our children to trust in God, we give them lasting strength.

I recall a recent moment with my 16-year-old daughter who had lost her phone on the bus. She came home panicked, nearly in tears, worried about her bank card inside the phone. But her immediate reaction was to sit beside me and pray. She asked God for a good Samaritan to find the phone and return it to the driver.

A week later, she called the bus company, and the phone had been found – completely intact, including the bank card. That moment touched me deeply. It showed that the reflex to turn to God in prayer had become natural for her. Instead of panicking or losing hope, she remained positive and took it to God. It was a beautiful testimony that I want to share to show how powerful it is to pass on faith to our children.

Raising children in faith also means modelling forgiveness, patience, and humility. We often receive compliments about our children – that they're polite, respectful, helpful, kind, and patient. One story I remember: after closing the salon late one evening, I offered to drive a client home. Without me saying anything, my daughter instinctively sat in the backseat, leaving the front seat for the client. The client later told me how deeply touched she was by that gesture – a simple act of respect that's becoming rare.

Of course, things aren't perfect. There are always challenges in raising children. Sometimes they're tired, resistant, or tempted to misbehave. But when God is at the centre, children know how to realign themselves. They remember the foundation that has been laid in their lives.

I grew up in a spiritual environment – I went to church, sang in the choir – and I thank God that my parents introduced me to that world from a young age. My husband had a similar upbringing. I was raised in a Catholic family before joining a more revival-based church, and my husband grew up Protestant, also very involved in church life. These spiritual roots shaped us as adults and helped us navigate our 17 years of marriage. We've learned to forgive, to be patient, to communicate – and it all began with the spiritual foundation we were given.

Over time, those small seeds of faith grow into deep roots. A home built on faith cultivates lasting trust, compassion, and resilience. Even when our children make mistakes, they know to come back and apologise. And we, as parents, also apologise when we've reacted too harshly. It's about relationship, communication, and mutual respect.

I'll close this chapter with **Joshua 24:15**:

"As for me and my house, we will serve the Lord."

May this vision guide every parent in their parenting journey. Teaching our children faith doesn't just lead to a joyful childhood – it builds strong adults and a lasting family legacy.

May God bless you abundantly

REFLECTIVE QUESTIONS

1. How present is faith in your daily family life?

Think about how often you pray together, talk about God, or reference biblical values at home.

2. In what ways are you modelling faith to your children?

Are your children learning to trust God by watching how you respond to challenges?

3. Have you seen any examples where your child's faith was evident in their actions?

Reflect on a moment where your child prayed, forgave, or acted with kindness inspired by faith.

4. How do you respond when your children make mistakes?

Do you create an environment of grace, patience, and correction rooted in love?

5. Do you have a family spiritual routine (e.g. prayer time, Bible reading, church attendance)?

If not, what small step can you take this week to establish one?

6. What faith-based values do you hope to leave as a legacy for your children?

Consider what you'd like your children to remember or carry into adulthood from their spiritual upbringing.

PRACTICAL EXERCISES

1. Create a Family Faith Routine

Choose one or two days a week to have a short devotion, prayer, or worship session as a family. Start simple – even 10 minutes is a good beginning.

2. Memory Verse of the Week

Pick a Bible verse (e.g. Proverbs 22:6 or Joshua 24:15) to memorise and reflect on together.

3. Testimony Time

Once a week, share testimonies as a family. Encourage each person (including children) to talk about something God did for them that week.

4. Faith in Action Challenge

Choose one small act of kindness or service your child can do, then reflect on how it ties back to biblical teaching (e.g. helping a sibling, sharing, praying for someone).

5. Gratitude Journal

Start a faith and gratitude journal with your children. Each evening, write or draw one thing they're thankful for and one thing they prayed about.

6. Prayer Wall or Jar

Create a space where your family can write prayer requests or praises and review them together over time to see answered.

7

The Power Of Connection And Communication

We've now come to Chapter Seven: the power of connection and communication. To summarise everything, it's impossible to succeed in your role as a parent without talking about connection. That connection, especially with the mother, begins as early as the umbilical cord. It lays the foundation. And that's something I love, because I was able to build a unique bond with each of my children from birth. That bond—those blessings, the doors that opened, and the grace that followed—was what inspired this book.

A strong relationship between parents and children relies on open communication. It's something we cultivate every day. I remember having open communication with my parents, especially my mother. My father was stricter, so there were things I couldn't tell him, but my mother would often insert herself into our conversations— "What are you talking about?" she'd ask. That openness allowed me to confide in her easily, and that's what I've also developed with my children.

I prefer that my children come and tell me when something difficult is happening so I can help, rather than them trying to handle it alone. Whether it's challenges at school, issues with friends, or navigating influence from others—I open the door for conversation. Even when it came to romantic interests, I've given advice to my older daughters on how to manage those emotions and situations.

Thanks to God, our eldest is now 24 years old, working, and thinking about marriage and having children, but she's focused on her career. She knows the values we've instilled, including how to approach love. Our second daughter is 19 and not in a relationship yet, but she shares with us what's on her mind. This has built a genuine connection and open dialogue with each of our children.

FOR EXAMPLE, around the dinner table—which used to be set for nine of us before our eldest moved to London—we take the time to talk, laugh, play games, and pray together. It has helped me detect issues early. I remember when my son was 13 and started hanging around kids who smoked. Because of our open communication, I noticed the signs quickly and was able to guide him away from that influence.

As parents, we must understand that external influence can easily steer a child off course. When we are present and take time to talk, listen, and look into their eyes, we can catch these things early. That's one of the difficulties many parents face—when there's no communication, children are easily influenced by negative peer groups, leading to problems at home.

There was a time I was being called to the school often because of my son's behaviour. The first step was to pray and then talk to him with love, explaining right from wrong. This created a climate of trust where he knew he could open up—even if it was something upsetting—and we would find a solution together.

Every child has a different personality, and it's up to us as parents to learn how to guide each one. That happens through communication, observation, and understanding what each child wants to express.

James 1:19 says, "Everyone should be quick to listen, slow to speak, and slow to become angry." This teaches us to listen patiently, creating space for our children to express themselves freely and develop emotional intelligence. It allows them to name and manage their emotions.

Connection is also built in the simple but meaningful moments—going to church, spending time with friends, holidays, cooking or helping at the shop. These daily acts—like sharing a meal, saying a bedtime prayer, or simply being present—build strong bonds. It's what I received from my parents and what my husband and I now pass on to our children.

As parents, we have the privilege to create a bond that reflects God's unconditional love.

As **1 Corinthians 13:7** says :

"Love bears all things, believes all things, hopes all things, endures all things."

Loving in this way creates a lifelong relationship that bears fruit over time. Even if you don't yet have children, it's still a blessing. It's a time to work on yourself, to grow, and be ready to receive that blessing. And if you're not yet in an environment with children, find ways to serve and learn—that experience will bless you when the time comes.

Looking back, I realise how much I served around children even before having my own. I helped friends with their children, held newborns for the first time, attended births, looked after nieces, nephews, cousins, and my younger sister. That service brought me grace —and I see today how I'm reaping that harvest.

Now, with a daughter aged 24, another at 19, then 16, a son of 15, a daughter of 13, a son of 11, and our youngest at 4, I can truly say: it's possible. We've succeeded, and it's a grace. It's not just the grace of having children, but the blessings that have followed—the financial doors that opened, the opportunities, the strength to become an entrepreneur—all tied to the arrival of our children.

Each child comes with a grace. Each child carries a talent. As parents, we get to discover those gifts and guide them. God equips us with everything we need to fulfil this mission of parenting. It's truly a win-win—a blessing for both the parents and the children.

So, I want to encourage every parent: love your children, be present with them, surround them with your attention, and build lasting connections. This is the beauty and heart of this book—to bless families and generations through this story.

May God bless you richly.

REFLECTIVE QUESTIONS

1. How would you describe the current communication between you and your child(ren)?

Is it open, strained, distant, or warm?

2. When was the last time your child came to you with a problem?

How did you respond? Would you respond differently now?

3. Do your children feel emotionally safe to express themselves around you?

What signs tell you they do or don't?

4. How often do you intentionally set aside time to

connect with your children without distractions (phones, TV, work)?

5. What conversations are you avoiding with your children that may be necessary for their growth?

6. What did you learn from your own parents about communication?

What do you want to repeat, and what would you like to do differently?

7. How well do you know the emotional and social world of each of your children?

Do you understand their friendships, fears, and dreams?

PRACTICAL EXERCISES

1. One-on-One Time

Set aside 15–30 minutes this week to spend one-on-one with each of your children. Let them choose the activity and use that time to listen without interruption.

2. Family Table Talk

Introduce a "High and Low" session at dinner: each person shares one good thing and one difficult thing from their day. This builds empathy and trust.

3. Weekly Check-In Journal

Give each child a small journal where they can write questions, thoughts, or things they find hard to say aloud. Read and respond privately once a week.

. . .

4. **Connection Over Correction**

For a week, focus more on connecting with your child before correcting them. Acknowledge their feelings first, then gently guide.

5. **Create a Communication Corner**

Choose a safe space in your home where children know they can speak to you honestly without fear of being judged or punished.

6. **Teach "Name It to Tame It"**

Help your child learn to name their emotions. Use an emotion chart or simple questions like "What are you feeling right now?" or "Where do you feel it in your body?"

7. **Read or Watch Together**

Choose a short story, Bible passage, or family movie to enjoy together. Afterward, discuss the characters' emotions, decisions, and what you learned.

About the Author

Sophie Bemba Kemoko a wife, mother of seven children, is a novelist, motivational speaker, business coach, and life coach specialising in family matters. She is a French citizen, originally from Congo-Brazzaville, and has resided in the United Kingdom since 2007. She is the CEO of several companies: **'COACHES D'EXCELLENCE'** , **'MSK MEDIA CONSULTING**, **'SK PRESTIGE HAIR AND BEAUTY ACADEMY'**. As an investor, she was motivated to write this book because she realised the blessing of becoming a parent, and above all, wanted to empower many parents who tend to neglect their parental mission. In her book, she shares her personal experiences as a mother of seven children through tips, secrets, testimonials, and practical advice, which could help parents and future parents to understand the mission behind parenthood. She hopes that this book will be able to help and create happy and fulfilled families, allowing both parents and children, to know their place, and know how to build strong and loving bonds.

Contact

Email: mskdigitalgroup@gmail.com.

https://mskbusinessmedia.com

.